IMAGES OF WAR
MALTA GC

IMAGES OF WAR
MALTA GC

RARE PHOTOGRAPHS FROM WARTIME ARCHIVES

JON SUTHERLAND AND
DIANE CANWELL

Pen & Sword
AVIATION

First published in Great Britain in 2009 by
PEN & SWORD AVIATION
an imprint of
Pen & Sword Books Ltd,
47 Church Street, Barnsley,
South Yorkshire.
S70 2AS

ISBN 978-1-84884-044-7

A CIP catalogue record for this book is available
from the British Library

Typeset by Mac Style, Beverley, East Yorkshire
Printed and bound in Great Britain by CPI

Pen & Sword Books Ltd incorporates the imprints of
Pen & Sword Aviation, Pen & Sword Maritime,
Pen & Sword Military, Pen & Sword Select, Pen & Sword Military Classics,
Leo Cooper, Wharncliffe Local History

For a complete list of Pen & Sword titles please contact:
PEN & SWORD BOOKS LIMITED
47 Church Street, Barnsley, South Yorkshire, S70 2AS, England.
E-mail: enquiries@pen-and-sword.co.uk
Website: www.pen-and-sword.co.uk

Contents

Dedication

To Sergeant William (Bill) John Lazell (1920–1980)
and to those who withstood the siege of Malta 1940–1943

Many thanks to Paul Lazell and his family.

Introduction

The island of Malta is literally situated at the crossroads of the Mediterranean. Incredibly, it suffered an ordeal of hunger, terror and bombardment at the hands of the Italians and Germans during the Second World War that would surpass almost any other in the war.

In a single 24-hour period on 20–21 March 1942, 295 tons of bombs fell on Ta' Qali airfield. This made Ta' Qali the most bombed allied airfield of the war. In April 1942, 6,728 tons of bombs fell on Malta, some thirty-six times the tonnage that devastated Coventry. In fact in March and April 1942 more bombs were dropped on Malta than fell on London during the entire Blitz. Overall, Malta suffered 154 days of continual raids compared to London's fifty-seven at the height of the Blitz.

Malta is almost at the heart of the Mediterranean, 1,100 miles east of Gibraltar and 911 miles west of Alexandria. However, it is closest to North Africa and to Sicily, being just 185 miles east of Tunisia and 200 miles from Tripoli. Sicily lies just 60 miles north. The most significant harbour in the Maltese islands is the Grand Harbour, on the eastern coast of Malta. In fact it is two harbours divided by a peninsula, dominated by the capital, Valletta. To the north of Valletta is Marsamxett, another harbour, and on the south coast is the only other harbour of any significance, Marsaxlokk.

Prior to the outbreak of the Second World War, Valletta had become the Royal Navy's Mediterranean Fleet Headquarters, although the headquarters was moved to Alexandria in Egypt at the beginning of the Second World War. By the time Italy declared war in June 1940 there were 300,000 civilians on the islands, fewer than 4,000 British troops, just over forty anti-aircraft guns, four Gladiators and three pilots, and just five weeks' food supplies.

Inevitably, Malta would become the focus of Italian attention in the Mediterranean. It was an isolated British colony, close to the Italian mainland. The Italians feared that it would be used by the British to launch attacks. It became one of Mussolini's priorities to beat the island into submission by air and pave the way for its occupation.

The events that would take place between June 1940 and the generally accepted end of the siege by air and sea in late 1942 would have few parallels during the Second World War. Ton for ton the Italians and the Germans dropped more bombs on Malta than the Luftwaffe had dropped on London during the Blitz. Almost daily there were interceptions and dogfights around and above the island. Hundreds of air alerts shattered the calm of the islands and sent civilians and military personnel alike scurrying for shelter. Hour by hour, the attrition on the island, its resources, population and often scant air cover threatened to overwhelm its ability to defend itself.

To begin with, the island's antiquated biplanes were all that stood in the way of the Italians flattening the island and forcing the civilians and the garrison into submission. Gradually, over the months, the Gladiators were reinforced by Hawker Hurricanes and then Spitfires and a host of other military aircraft, until defence became offence and it was the Italians and the Germans who would be subjected to incessant bombing and attack.

On 15 April 1942 King George VI awarded the island the George Cross. It was an award that was usually given to individuals, rather than a whole population, as the monarch said:

> To honour her brave people, I award the George Cross to the Island Fortress of Malta to bear witness to a heroism and devotion that will long be famous in history.

Undoubtedly Malta was one of the most intensively bombed areas during the Second World War. There were around 3,000 raids, nearly 1,500 civilians were killed and nearly 3,700 injured. It is notoriously difficult to be certain as to the aircraft losses on either side. The Royal Air Force claimed around 860 Italian and German aircraft, although this figure may, in fact, be closer to 600. Around 290 Spitfires and Hurricanes were lost between June 1940 and December 1942, although in all over 840 allied aircraft were lost, both in the air and on land. The German Luftwaffe claimed over 440 allied aircraft shot down.

The siege of Malta was conducted almost entirely by air. In the period up to the end of 1940, air activities were almost exclusively Italian. However, by early 1941, matching the fortunes of the Germans in North Africa, the Luftwaffe had reinforced the Italians and made a determined attempt to overwhelm the island's defences. With the changing fortunes in North Africa and Germany's obsession with the invasion of Russia, there was a lull before the Luftwaffe returned in 1942 and all but overwhelmed Malta's scant defences and pounded the island almost at will.

After April 1942 it was the allies who were on the offensive, intercepting aircraft attacks even before they crossed the coast. Rommel's supply vessels were intercepted daily and destroyed by aircraft operating out of Malta. No German or Italian vessel was safe along the whole of the African coast or from Italy to Greece.

Just prior to the launching of Montgomery's much-awaited North African Offensive at El Alamein, the Luftwaffe returned for one last time to overwhelm Malta. They assembled half of their bomber strength in the Mediterranean. By now, sufficient reinforcements had arrived on Malta, and the island held out as the Eighth Army drove along the North African coast, overrunning German airbases.

By the end of 1942 the siege was over and the island could now be turned into an offensive arm of the allied effort against the Italian mainland. Aircraft from the island covered the amphibious invasion of Sicily and continued to be instrumental in ensuring air superiority across the whole of the Mediterranean.

Lieutenant General Sir William Dobbie wrote in 1944 of the victory, which would have appeared to have been so impossible in 1940:

It was my privilege to witness these amazing happenings from the vantage point of Malta, which was destined to play a great part in the epic struggle. It is possible that the importance and the role of that island fortress have only been imperfectly understood until recently, but it is very evident now that its importance was so great and its role so vital to our wellbeing in the Mediterranean that its retention in our hands justified any effort and any sacrifice, however great. It is no exaggeration to say that the security of Malta reacted very definitely on the safety of Egypt, and all that those words imply. If Malta had fallen, the safety of Egypt would have been very gravely endangered. It was from Malta that the attacks were launched by sea and air on the enemy's lines of communication between Italy and North Africa. By means of these attacks we were able to exert some influence on the effectiveness of the enemy forces in North Africa, and in this way to reduce the threat on Egypt.

Dobbie went on to describe the perilous position that Malta found itself in at the beginning of hostilities:

Our resources were meagre enough. Especially in the early months of the Italian war, the garrison was unbelievably weak both in men and material, and the enemy undoubtedly knew exactly how weak we were. Our air resources on Malta were practically nil, although the fortress was only a few minutes flying away from the many air bases in Sicily and southern Italy at the disposal of the strong Regia Aeronautica. No wonder the Italians had been boasting that they would overrun the island within a few days of the declaration of war. Their resources were amply adequate to justify them making the attempt, especially in view of our own weakness. But this attempt was never made (just as the attempt to invade Britain was never made), and all other attempts during the two long years and more to reduce the fortress by other means failed. We acknowledge with admiration and gratitude the way the people of Malta, the three fighting services and the Merchant Navy faced the ordeal and willingly paid the price needed to keep Malta safe. But even so the fact that Malta is today still in British hands is a miracle. The miracle of Malta is a part, and a big part, of the Mediterranean miracle.

On 24 July 1941 members of the 7th Heavy Anti-Aircraft Regiment (7 HAA Regt), Royal Artillery, arrived on Malta. Among them was Sergeant William (Bill) John Lazell, then aged 21. Indeed, Bill was fortunate, if that is the right word, to be posted to Malta and to withstand the raids. When they arrived at Gibraltar, they boarded HMS *Manxman*. This was part of a large convoy which then effectively split in two. One half was sent to Singapore. The majority of those troops were captured by the Japanese and became prisoners of war. Bill would spend the next two years dodging bombs and shells.

Bill's battalion saw active service for the first time on Tuesday, 5 August 1941. The battalion would spend the next four years on Malta, where they endured some of the heaviest bombing raids in history. Bill captured the daily events in his diaries. He also took literally hundreds of photographs with his 35mm camera. Bill spent most of his time plotting formations of enemy aircraft and guiding in squadrons of RAF aircraft. Whenever he had the chance, though, he would man the twin Lewis guns and fire at any low-flying aircraft.

The regiment left Malta on Sunday, 5 March 1944 and Bill was reunited with his fiancée, Joy, and they married on Saturday, 12 August 1944. Bill saw further service in the Orkneys until the end of the war. Following his demobilization, Bill and Joy had three children, two daughters and son. It is his son, Paul, who we are indebted to for allowing us to use his late father's photographs. His wonderful collection of photographs and his extensive diaries remain an amazing historical account of the events on Malta. They also serve as a tribute to the men from all the armed services as well as the islanders involved.

Chapter One

The War in the Air

From small beginnings, just three Gloster Gladiators defended the skies above Malta against the Italian air force. As the months passed, Malta received a bewildering selection of aircraft and hastily assembled crews to hold the line against the growing aerial threat over the islands. A series of dangerous and audacious reinforcement missions out of Gibraltar would sustain the island's often tenuous ability to defend itself. At times the scant defenders would face as many as 100 enemy aircraft; swirling dogfights were a daily occurrence.

But as the months passed, with reinforcements of Hurricanes and Spitfires, the tide would turn and the skies over the islands were no longer safe for the invaders. Had the air war over the islands been lost and the sea around Malta become too hot for the Royal Navy then undoubtedly an invasion would have been launched, either by sea or by air.

For months the fate of the islands lay in the balance, with the British desperately juggling their limited resources in the Mediterranean between competing demands on a number of fronts. As the Spitfires came into the islands in May 1941 the Germans and the Italians would find the skies a terrifying place. Dozens of Spitfires and Hurricanes would be there to meet them.

Although the air war over Malta is typified by the Spitfire, great work was carried out by a range of other aircraft, including Beaufighters, Mosquitos, Liberators, Swordfish and Kittyhawks.

According to the official statistics, the number of enemy aircraft destroyed between the outbreak of war in 1939 and June 1943 in operations against the Royal Air Force and the Fleet Air Arm amounted to 3,500 in the Middle East region, which included Malta. This was an incredible total since the number of enemy aircraft shot down over Great Britain in the same period was 4,201. The RAF losses alone in the Middle East region, however, amounted to 1,977 aircraft.

Seen at Luqa, Hurricane Serial No. Z4544 fitted with long-range fuel tanks. This Hurricane was part of the third production batch of 1,700 aircraft built by Gloster Aircraft Co., to contract 85730/40/23a. It was powered by Rolls-Royce Merlin III or Rolls-Royce Merlin XX engines, driving Rotol or de Havilland three-blade variable-pitch propellers. The aircraft were delivered between July 1940 and August 1941, the average rate of production four to five aircraft per day.

In 1939 it was felt that the RAF needed a supplementary airfield in addition to the seaplane base at Kalafrana and the two other airfields at Hal Far and Ta' Qali. It was believed that a new airfield would solve some of the poor-weather problems that affected the other bases. Luqa was designed as an all-weather airfield. The site of the airfield was some 250 foot (76 metres) above sea level a mile and a half from the Grand Harbour and in hilly terrain. The area was also dotted with working quarries. Construction began in 1935 and it was to have three main tarmac runways with a fourth that remained without a surface until 1941.

Hurricane Z4941 was engaged in a dogfight on 4 September 1941. Some nineteen Macchi MC.200s of 10° Gruppo set off from Comiso led by Tenente Colonnello Carlo Romagnoli. They had been tasked to look for a ship that had been claimed to have been sunk by Ju 87s of 101° Gruppo. The MC.200s were some nine or ten miles off Malta, heading back to Sicily, when they were engaged by a number of Hurricanes. The British had scrambled twelve aircraft from No. 126 Squadron and nine from No. 185 Squadron. They spotted the Italian aircraft at 22,500 feet. Squadron Leader Rabagliati (Hurricane Z4941/XL) attacked two Macchis. One was immediately shot down.

No. 46 Squadron's ground crews reached Egypt early in July 1941. The squadron's pilots were operating in the defence of Malta, first as No. 46 Squadron, but later they were absorbed into No. 126 Squadron. They were almost constantly in action, claiming the destruction of nearly forty enemy aircraft, ten of them German and the remainder Italian.

This Hurricane was the victim of a ground attack in 1942. The first Hurricanes arrived on Malta on 28 June 1941. They were actually *en route* to the Middle East, but the Air Officer Commanding Malta, Air Commodore Sammy Maynard, persuaded the Air Ministry to let four of them stay. In July more Hurricanes arrived via the aircraft carrier HMS *Argus*. The Hurricanes would soon become the principal fighter defence force, operating out of Luqa airfield, which overlooked the Grand Harbour. In November 1941 nine of fourteen Hurricanes that lifted off from HMS *Argus* ran out of fuel due to a strong head wind before they reached Malta. In early 1942 the first Mark II Hurricanes were flown to Malta from HMS *Ark Royal* in the belief that they would be more than a match for the German Bf109. Initially there were no protective pens for the Hurricanes, but it was decided that they would be built around the edge of Luqa airfield. It was back-breaking work, with the pens being built with limestone blocks, four-gallon fuel cans filled with sand, and sandbags. A Wellington pen would need 60,000 filled fuel cans. RAF ground crew, Maltese civilians and soldiers from the garrison all lent a hand.

A Hurricane, smashed up and burning at Ta' Qali airfield in 1942. The airfield was built on the bed of an old lake. Before the war the airfield had been extensively used by an Italian civil airline. By 1940, the obstructions had been placed around the airfield to deter airborne landings. In October 1940, Wing Commander J R O'Sullivan and a small HQ staff began preparations for the creation of a single-squadron fighter station on the airfield. On 8 November, the airfield became RAF Station Ta' Qali. No. 261 Squadron moved in from Luqa and on 16 May 1941, Wing Commander J Warfield took over as Station Commander. Soon afterwards, No. 249 Squadron replaced No. 261 Squadron. No. 249 Squadron was to be the top-scoring squadron on Malta and would claim the 1,000th enemy kill over the island. The airfield is now the home of the Malta Aviation Museum.

At the Zebbug position on Gozo, in August 1942. The so-called 'Mad Spitfire' flies over, watched to the left of the picture by Bill Lazell. Zebbug is perched on two adjoining hilltops. It is the highest village on the island and therefore ideal for a radar post. Zebbug is some two miles (3.5km) away from Victoria, the capital of Gozo, nearby, and is the now the popular seaside resort of Marsalforn. Zebbug gains its name from the Maltese meaning, 'olives' or 'olive trees'.

In June 1943 Zebbug would have a more regal visitor, this time in the shape of King George VI. He paid a visit to the island on 20 June, after having also visited Malta.

In June 1943 work began on Gozo to build a new airfield that would be used by the United States Army Air Force. It was completed in just eighteen days, and on 23 June the first Spitfires of 31 Fighter Group, USAAF landed there, ferried in from Tunisia.

A de Havilland Mosquito at Luqa airfield in 1943. The Mosquito was originally designed as a twin-engine day-bomber, with the ability to outrun enemy fighters. It had no heavy defensive armament and due to its construction, using laminated ply and balsa, it was known as the 'Wooden Wonder'. At bases such as Luqa it was used as a day- or night-fighter, a fighter-bomber, pathfinder, intruder, photo-reconnaissance aircraft and for attacks on enemy shipping.

Mosquitos replaced the outclassed Bristol Beaufighters and saw action in nearly all theatres. Some 7,781 Mosquitos were produced. The last airworthy Mosquito crashed at an air show in the 1990s. Arguably, the Mosquito was the most versatile aircraft used in the Second World War. It was capable of speeds of around 400mph (644km/h) and could carry a bomb load of up to 4,000lb (1,814kg). The remains of a Mosquito have been found near Kalafrana.

The first Mosquito fighter unit to see action in the Mediterranean and Italy was No. 23 Squadron. They arrived in late December 1942. One of the top pilots was Wing Commander Peter G Wykeham-Barnes, who had already scored twelve kills in Hurricanes and Gladiators. He added two kills in 1943, flying DZ230. His aircraft was subsequently written off when it overshot a landing at Luqa on 22 June 1943.

Several Hurricanes line up for take-off at Ta' Qali airfield on Malta. A number of squadrons operated out of Ta' Qali airfield during the Second World War. These aircraft probably belong to No. 249 Squadron, who were shifted from North Weald in May 1941 and were re-equipped with Spitfires in February 1942. Their Hurricanes were flown to the island from HMS *Ark Royal* in June 1941. The squadron had successfully taken part in the Battle of Britain, with many of the pilots fully prepared for the arduous posting on Malta, having flown four or more missions each day.

A Hawker Hurricane IIA is in the process of being restored at the Malta Aviation Museum at Ta' Qali. Each year Ta' Qali airfield hosts part of the Malta International Air Show. Visiting Hawker Hurricanes are welcome guests.

A Hudson operating out of Malta in 1942. The Hudson, built by Lockheed, was the military version of the Electra. It was later supplied to the Commonwealth and to other services. Some versions of the aircraft were used as anti-submarine aircraft by the Fleet Air Arm, although this aircraft is possibly from No. 233 Squadron, RAF, which was operating out of Malta and Gibraltar in 1942. In the Mediterranean the Hudsons were particularly successful against enemy U-boats. No. 233 Squadron claimed its first U-boat kill in May 1942, with the sinking of *U-573*. A large number of the aircraft were delivered on a lend-lease basis to the RAF and a smaller number to the Royal Navy. The Hudson had a crew of five and was a versatile aircraft. Built in the USA, it had a maximum speed of 246mph (396km/h). On 8 October 1939, over Jutland, an RAF Hudson was the first British aircraft to shoot down a German aircraft.

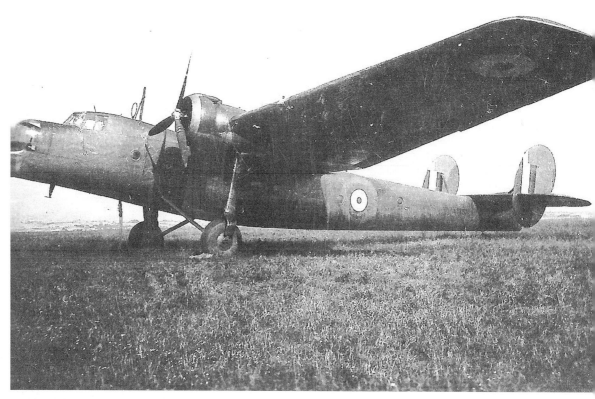

A Bristol Bombay at Luqa airfield. Only eighty of these aircraft were ordered and the first aircraft were not delivered until 1939. The last thirty ordered were cancelled because the plane was obsolete by European standards and was primarily used as a transport aircraft. It was in Bristol Bombays belonging to No. 216 Squadron that the Greek royal family was evacuated from Crete to Egypt. It was also in a Bombay that Lieutenant General William Henry Ewart 'Strafer' Gott lost his life on 7 August 1942. He had hitched a lift in the unarmed transport plane for a return trip to Cairo from the front lines. The aircraft was shot down by a fighter flown by Emil Clade. The pilot of the Bombay, Jimmy James, then a sergeant, survived the attack and was later awarded the Distinguished Flying Cross for his attempts to save the passengers and crew.

An RAF Douglas Boston (A-20) on Malta. It saw service with the Fleet Air Arm, but primarily with the RAF, where it was used as a night intruder. Production of the aircraft was stopped in September 1944, by which time over 7,000 had been built. The Bostons were supplied to Nos. 13, 14, 18, 55 and 114 Squadrons operating in the Middle East from 1941. The aircraft had a maximum speed of 311mph (500km/h) at sea level and 338mph (544km/h) at 12,500 feet (3,810m). Its cruising speed was 273mph (439km/h). Carrying a 1,000lb (435kg) bomb load it had a range of 745 miles (1,199km) but with double the bomb load this was reduced to 525 miles (845km). It had a crew of four and was protected by a pair of Browning machine-guns in a flexible dorsal position, four additional Brownings in the nose and a Vickers machine-gun in a ventral position.

The remains of a Fairey Swordfish, which was the main torpedo bomber of the Fleet Air Arm during the early years of the Second World War. Originally thirteen squadrons were used by the Fleet Air Arm, eleven of which served on the five fleet carriers. The Swordfish's best-known exploit was at Taranto when they launched a torpedo attack on the Italian fleet. At its peak the Swordfish was in use in twenty-six squadrons and was still being used by nine of them in 1945. The Mark I of this aircraft was flown in 1934, and was designed as a three-man torpedo bomber and reconnaissance biplane. Its wings were capable of being folded back for better storage on aircraft carriers. Generally the aircraft was considered too slow to cope with the punishment it could expect from enemy anti-aircraft fire. The Mark II was introduced in 1943 and the Mark III later in the same year. By this time the focus was on anti-submarine radar. Production of this aircraft ended in 1944 but by this time the Swordfish was being used as a minelayer, for anti-submarine warfare, for convoy escorts and as a torpedo bomber. It had a maximum speed of 138mph (222km/h) and a range of just over 1,000 miles (1,609km). In all some 2,391 of the aircraft were built. The Malta-based Swordfish were a continual irritation for German and Italian shipping. Many of the aircraft had already operated in France and were transferred to the Mediterranean theatre. On 22 August 1940 three Swordfish attacked Italian warships in the Libyan port of Bomba Bay. They destroyed two submarines, a submarine tender and a destroyer, amazingly with just three torpedoes. The destroyer blew up when its tender exploded.

This is an RAF photograph of a Malta-based Blenheim, taken while it was observing a burning Axis vessel off the coast of Malta. The Blenheim was extensively used by a number of squadrons based at various times on Malta, including Nos 82, 105, 107, 110, and 139, as well as Coastal Command No. 69 Squadron. The wreck of one RAF Bristol Blenheim is a major attraction for divers some 42 metres (138 feet) under the water off the coast of Malta. It is extremely well preserved, with both engines and wings intact. The rear fuselage separated from the plane when it impacted over sixty years ago. The Blenheim was essential in the war of attrition against the German and Italian supply convoys heading for North Africa. When the major German and Italian attacks were made on Malta in early 1942 the Blenheim was withdrawn to Egypt and left Malta on 22 February 1942.

These Beaufighters are seen sitting on Luqa airfield in 1943. The Beaufighter was primarily used by Coastal Command Squadrons. No. 227 Squadron, which had been formed from a detachment of No. 235 Squadron in August 1942, operated from Luqa. A detachment of No. 252 Squadron operated for a brief period in August 1942 from Luqa, but the longest-staying squadron with Beaufighters, No. 272 Squadron, operated out of Ta' Qali and Luqa between the beginning of November 1942 and the beginning of June 1943.

On 17 March 1943 at around 11.25 hours, nine Beaufighters belonging to No. 272 Squadron scrambled to escort nine Beauforts belonging to No. 39 Squadron, to attack enemy shipping. Thirteen minutes later Sergeant Donald Frazee, piloting the aircraft, and Sergeant Sandery, his observer, ran into problems. The aircraft began to vibrate and lose speed. They ditched the Beaufighter into the sea 3,280 feet (1,000m) off Dragonara Point at Sliema. The aircraft hit the water at 100mph (161km/h). The crew managed to get out and they were picked up by RAF Air-Sea Rescue launch HSL166. The wreckage of the aircraft can still be seen in less than 131 feet (40m) of water in the mouth of St Julian's Bay.

This wreckage is that of a Beaufighter at Luqa in 1942. Such was the perilous shortage of spares that any salvageable part, particularly from the engines, was scavenged from even the most unpromising of wrecks. This group of RAF mechanics are busy at work salvaging engine spares from this write-off. The first Beaufighters to operate from Malta worked with No. 252 Squadron from May 1941. Later No. 108 Squadron also used the aircraft. The Beaufighter was a natural replacement for the Blenheim IV. In all, the Beaufighter would serve with fifty-nine squadrons in both Fighter Command and Coastal Command, as well as squadrons in the Middle East and the Far East. It had a maximum speed of 303mph (488km/h), a range of just less than 1,500 miles (2,214km) and surface ceiling of 15,000 feet (4,572m). For protection it had four machine-guns in the nose and one in the rear cockpit.

This rather more intact Beaufighter is seen sitting beside the runway at Luqa airfield in 1942. Almost certainly this would have been an aircraft belonging to either of No. 227, No. 248 or No. 272 Squadron. In many respects the Bristol Beaufighter was the epitome of British improvisation. It was originally designed as a heavy long-range fighter, and later it was modified to become a general reconnaissance and torpedo bomber, which was primarily used by Coastal Command. It was also ideal against night attacks. When production ceased in September 1945 some 5,562 Beaufighters had been produced.

A Curtiss P-40 Kittyhawk, which had first seen combat in June 1941. Kittyhawks and Spitfire Vs were taken to Malta in order to tip the balance against the Bf109s, which were often seen as superior to the Hurricanes. The British often referred to the Kittyhawk as the Tomahawk. It was inferior to the Spitfire, except at low altitude and in its slightly tougher structure. Nonetheless in times of need it was used as an escort fighter and fought against Bf109s and Macchi MC.202s. It was a development of the earlier Tomahawk and was used extensively in the Mediterranean, North Africa and Malta from around 1942. Some 3,000 of them were used by Commonwealth air forces.

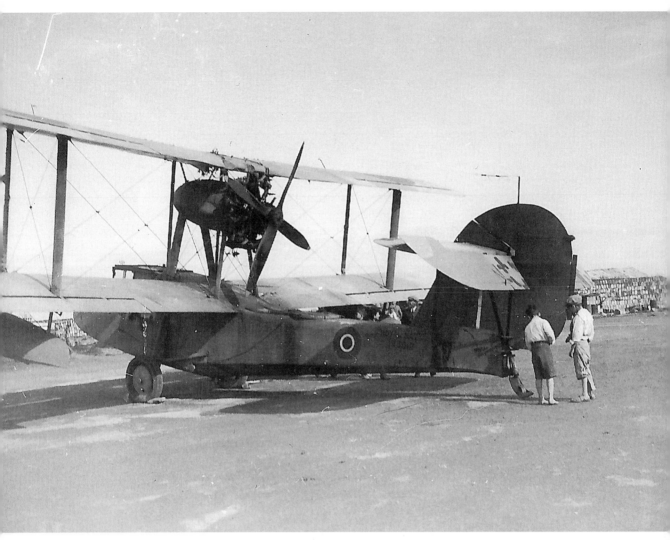

This Walrus is seen at Luqa in 1943. This aircraft may have belonged to Coastal Command No. 248 Squadron, which was based at Hal Far during July 1943, although close inspection reveals that it is in fact a Royal Navy Walrus. These aircraft were amphibians and were invaluable in picking up downed crew and were extensively used by the RAF Air-Sea Rescue Service. It was a Supermarine aircraft that was designed to be launched by catapult with a full load. Some 740 were built between 1936 and 1944. The Walrus was both shore-based and catapult-launched, primarily from capital ships. There were at least five confirmed enemy submarines sunk or damaged by Walruses during the Second World War. Only three of the aircraft survive to this day; two are in Britain and one is in Australia.

Bill Lazell marked this photograph as a Sunderland being shot up in Kalafrana Bay, but in fact it may well be a Sunderland that was hit in St Paul's Bay on 6 March 1941. In the engagement Sergeant Alan Jones, firing a Vickers machine-gun, tried to beat the fighters off, but was shot and killed. German Me110s returned on 10 March and managed to set the Sunderland on fire. The blaze got out of control and the flying boat was towed into Mistra Bay, where it eventually sank.

In the first two weeks of July 1943 the Short Sunderlands of No. 230 Squadron were attached to rescue duties. They worked in co-operation with Walruses of No. 284 Squadron, operating out of Hal Far. Malta was a major component in the Air-Sea Rescue Service for Operation Husky, because by this time over thirty-five squadrons were based on the island. The vessels used by the ASR had now risen to eight high-speed launches (HSLs), six seaplane tenders and four pinnaces. Invariably Sunderlands were escorted by P-38 Lightnings. On one occasion on 17 July, in the sea to the south-west of Naples, there was a report of no less than seven dinghies. Sunderlands came in but were driven off by enemy aircraft. On the following morning a Sunderland managed to pick up six aircrew. Another returned to search, this time escorted by P-38s. They ran into fifteen German Ju 52 transports and shot them all down.

A Martin Maryland, probably based at Luqa airfield. On 6 September 1940 three American-built Martin Marylands touched down after a seven-hour flight from Britain. They had flown overnight across enemy-occupied France, photographing Sardinia on their way. The Marylands will forever be associated with Adrian Warburton. His father had been a submarine commander based at Malta in the First World War and Adrian had been christened on his submarine in the Grand Harbour. Adrian was something of a misfit; he had arrived on Malta under the command of the Australian 'Tich' Whiteley to form No. 431 Reconnaissance Flight. During his time on Malta Warburton flew innumerable photo-reconnaissance missions over enemy-held territory, earning the Marylands the title 'The Diehards'. On 1 October 1943 Warburton took command of No. 336 Photo Reconnaissance Wing at La Marsa, in North Africa. Soon afterwards he was badly injured in a motoring accident in Tunis and sent back to Britain. But he was itching for action and, accompanied by an American pilot, he took off in a P-38 on 12 April 1944 to carry out photo-reconnaissance over Schweinfurt, when he disappeared. The wreckage of the P-38 was found near Comiso in Sicily.

This photograph shows the wreckage of Adrian Warburton's favourite Maryland, AR733. Notice the numerous holes at the rear of the fuselage, where it had been shot up by flak and enemy aircraft over its target. This Maryland sustained damage on 12 February 1942 when it was attacked by Bf109s near Pantelleria island. The gunner occupying the top turret was killed and Sergeant Robert Watson, occupying the belly turret, was severely wounded. Watson held off an Bf109 and shot it down before putting out the fire in the aircraft. The pilot made a forced landing due to the failure of the elevators and the tail being shot away. Watson was later awarded the Distinguished Flying Medal.

This Maryland is seen sitting in a safety pen at Luqa airfield. These pens were created to protect the precious aircraft and service vehicles. When an aircraft landed the ground crew would carry a numbered sign and the pilot would follow them into the safety pen for refuelling and rearming. This would allow them to get back into the air as quickly as possible to prevent the Germans or Italians from destroying the aircraft on the ground.

The Maryland was a twin-engine monoplane with a crew of three and a top speed of 310mph (982km/h). Around 450 of the aircraft were built. Few of them saw any real combat; particularly those used by the Fleet Air Arm, but the RAF used them for photo-reconnaissance operations. It was a Maryland bomber that took the photographs before and after the attack on the Italian fleet at Taranto on 11 November 1940. The British had acquired the bulk of the French Martin Marylands. Between December 1940 and April 1941, 150 Maryland IIs were delivered to the RAF. The Maryland was also used by the British and the South Africans as a light bomber in north-west Africa until 1941.

This Vickers Wellington probably came to grief on 2 April 1942. The Wellington (BB512) was being delivered by Overseas Aircraft Delivery Unit (OADU) when it collided on the flare path with a Wellington (Z8575) of No. 1443 Flight from Harwell. Subsequently, another unnamed Wellington ran into the wreckage of one of these Wellingtons at the side of the runway while taking off and was burned out, but fortunately there were no injuries.

The Vickers Wellington was originally designed in the mid-1930s and was used as a night bomber, but ultimately it was replaced by the Avro Lancaster. Nonetheless, it continued to be used in a variety of roles, including anti-submarine warfare. It had a bewildering number of variants, including bombers, coastal command, transport, trainers and conversion variants. In all, Wellingtons flew over 47,000 operations for Bomber Command alone. Losses of the aircraft were 1,332 of the 11,461 of all versions that were built until production ceased in October 1945.

This is another view of the Wellington crash of April 1942. On 4 November 1940 another Wellington had crashed onto the roof of a house, trapping the occupants, two adults and five children. The Wellington then broke in two and half of it fell down a 40ft (12m) shaft. Constable Carmel Camilleri of the Malta Police was later given the George Medal for entering the shaft to help rescue the trapped airmen.

An Italian air force Cant Z.506 torpedo plane in St Paul's Bay; notice the seaplane tender close by. Bill Lazell identifies this as a Cant that was forced to land after being hit by anti-aircraft fire, but it may be the one that was involved in an incident that took place on 29 July 1942, when a Beaufort crew that had been taken prisoner-of-war in Greece were being ferried in the Cant to Italy. They overpowered the Italian crew and headed for Malta. Spitfires came in to attack and one of the Beaufort crew waved his white vest out of an open window. As the Cant touched down on the water between Sliema and St Paul's Bay it ran out of fuel. The Cant was later towed by the seaplane tender (ST253) into the Grand Harbour and it was later used for Air-Sea Rescue duties.

The bizarre incident took place on 29 July. The episode had begun the previous day off Sapienza in southern Greece:

The captain of the aircraft [a Beaufort] was Lieutenant E T Strever of Klerksdorp, South Africa; the rest of the crew were Pilot Officer (now Flying Officer) W M Dunsmore of Maghull, near Liverpool, Sergeant J A Wilkinson of Auckland, and Sergeant A R Brown of Timaru, both from New Zealand. After releasing his torpedo at a merchant vessel, and being badly shot up by flack, Strever realised that his aircraft was doomed. As it hit the sea, he went under, but somehow managed to clamber clear of the wreckage and join the crew in their dinghy. Ninety seconds later the aircraft sank. After paddling for some time towards the coast, they saw an Italian float plane [a Cant Z.506B], which presently landed about 100 yards away. Strever swam over to it and was courteously received with a brandy and a cigarette; he then explained in pantomime what had happened. The rest of the crew was picked up, and the Cant float plane taxied to a nearby island [Preveza in Greece]. Here, after a hearty meal, they were given the run of the officers' mess for the rest of the day. In the evening they had another excellent meal with the Italian officers, who considerately gave up their rooms to the crew when bedtime arrived. The only sense of imprisonment was that the guards were posted in the passage and outside their windows. In the morning, after a breakfast of eggs and coffee specially provided for them, and having been photographed with their captors, the crew were taken aboard the Cant again, which then set off for Taranto. The Cant's crew consisted of a pilot, second pilot, engineer, wireless-operator-observer and a corporal acting as an armed escort. Wilkinson was the first to see an opportunity of capturing the aircraft. Attracting the observer's attention, he hit him on the jaw and seized the escort's revolver. Passing this to Strever, he then used the corporal's body as a shield in approaching the first pilot. Strever followed, brandishing the escort's pistol, and held up the pilot before he could get at his own weapon. The Italian had put the aircraft's nose down as though to land, but at a menacing sign from Strever he changed his mind and pulled the stick back again. Meanwhile Dunsmore and Brown dealt with the rest of the crew and Strever took over the controls. The capture of the aircraft took only a few seconds, but Strever was now faced with the difficulty of having no maps or charts, and of not knowing the speed or capacity of the aircraft, nor how much petrol would be needed to reach Malta. He therefore set the second pilot free and put him at the controls. After making rough and ready calculations of his own, Strever decided that if they could not reach Malta they would come down in Sicily and trust to luck. The Italian steered the course set for him and Strever himself took the controls from time to time. At length they hit the toe of Italy, which enabled him to get some sort of fix, and he decided to chance the petrol situation and head for Malta. As they approached the island there began the most terrifying episode of the trip. While flying at deck level, three Spitfires attacked them. Brown spun the guns about to show the fighters that he was not going to fire, and Dunsmore took off his white vest and trailed it out of the cockpit as a sign of surrender. But still the Spitfires spat, and when one of the wings was hit by machine-guns and cannons, Strever ordered the Italian to come down on the water. As they did so the engines stopped. They had run out of petrol.

The Air Battle of Malta: the Official Account of the RAF in Malta, June 1940 to November 1942, HMSO, 1944, pp. 77–8.

The Cant had come down between Sliema and St Paul's Bay about two miles offshore. Initially it was towed in by HSL107 and then a seaplane tender took over to bring it into St Paul's pier. The Air-Sea Rescue men were amazed to see the Beaufort crew and their Italian prisoners. The war might have been over for the Italians, but it was not over for the Cant. The Italian insignia was over-painted with British roundels and it was pressed into service as a floatplane for Air-Sea Rescue. Strever personally supervised the Italians and felt that he had to return their hospitality in some way. Through a translator they agreed that there was nothing personal about what had happened and that they fully understood. In order to extend the fraternal spirit, Strever and the crew shared a bottle of wine with the Italians, which he had been hoarding to take with him on leave.

An Bf109 that had pancaked at Luqa after having been hit by Bill Lazell's anti-aircraft battery. As soon as the air raid was over and he was given permission to leave his post Bill rushed over to Luqa to make sure he had a photograph of this historic event. The aircraft is probably from Jagdgeschwader 53, which was engaged against Malta in the early months of 1942. The unit was led by Major Günther von Maltzahn and included notable pilots, such as Herbert Kaminski, Freidrich-Karl 'Tutti' Müller, Herbert Rollwage and Wolfe-Dietrich Wilcke.

Another Bf109, burning furiously during the major Luftwaffe offensive against Malta in 1942. German and Italian losses were so heavy in 1942 that by October they had effectively conceded defeat. In any case, the priorities for the Germans in particular had changed and pilots were now needed on the Russian front against overwhelming numbers of Russian aircraft. Time after time the experienced Bf109 and Bf110 pilots tried to knock out Malta's three airfields and Valletta harbour, but they came up against determined opposition, in the shape of the air defence of aircraft and anti-aircraft guns.

This is yet another stricken Bf109 from the 1942 period. Early 1942 was a dark time for Malta. The islands were more isolated than ever before, with the Eighth Army in retreat in North Africa. Day after day the Germans mounted heavy raids against the islands, knocking out aircraft on the ground and killing Maltese civilians and military personnel. On 15 February 1942 alone the Germans launched 120 Ju 88s and fifty Bf109s against Luqa.

Chapter Two

The Ground Defence

The heroics of the fighter pilots and the unstinting efforts of the ground crews would not have been enough to save Malta in the dark days of the air siege. Across the island anti-aircraft units from the Royal Artillery and from the Royal Malta Artillery were on constant watch for raiders. Radar played a vital role in air alerts, tracking enemy formations and guiding in fighter cover to intercept. Often the anti-aircraft positions came under direct attack from either Stukas or fighters and bombers machine-gunning at low altitude.

The Royal Artillery and the Royal Malta Artillery, commanded between May 1941 and December 1942 by Major General C T Beckett, played an enormous role against almost impossible odds. Sometimes the guns fired until their barrels were red-hot or worn out; often they ran out of ammunition or were restricted in how many rounds they could fire because of shortages. They threw up a protective barrage over harbours and installations; sometimes it seemed that it would be impossible for an enemy aircraft to penetrate. At night the sky was pierced by bright-red shots from Bofors guns, tracer rounds and searchlights.

The Royal Corps of Signals struggled to keep communications around the island in order. Lines were frequently severed by the bombing. Delayed-action bombs were always a threat. Other defenders, armed with just Lewis guns or Bren guns, tried to knock the enemy raiders out of the skies.

This is the Operations Room in the Lascaris Bastion at Valletta. The Operations Room was well protected underground and was the RAF Fighter Control for No. 8 Sector. The names of the guns and radar positions can be seen in the picture, along with the pilot IDs.

A number of Maltese women and WAAFs worked in the Operations Room in Valletta throughout the siege. In May 1943 Group Captain Miller was in overall charge of the Operations Room. A version of the Operations Room was featured in the 1953 movie, *The Malta Story*, starring Alec Guinness and Jack Hawkins.

A Bofors position in the Grand Harbour, seen in 1943. At the beginning of the war a decision had been made to increase the anti-aircraft defences on Malta and at the outbreak there were thirty-four heavy guns and eight Bofors guns. Approval had been given to increase this to 122 heavy guns, 60 light guns and 24 searchlights, but by June 1940 only the searchlights had been delivered.

A defensive position near the Grand Harbour, as a convoy arrives. By 1942 heavy anti-aircraft defences had increased to five regiments, with 112 guns deployed in 29 positions. Many of the positions had either two or four guns.

A twin Lewis gun anti-aircraft position at Marsa. Marsa had extensive playing fields and a race course belonging to the United Services Sports Club. There was very little cover, yet it was home to the Royal West Kent Regiment. On 26 June 1940 Italian bombers had jettisoned their bombs over Marsa and an incendiary bomb had hit a bus, killing twenty-one passengers and injuring nine others.

A Bofors position at the Grand Harbour, taken in 1943. The Bofors guns were capable of firing 160 rounds a minute. They had a crew of six; four of the men passed ammunition in clips of four 1.5in (40mm) shells. The other two men were detailed to train the gun on the target and fire. The gun had a range of some four miles. Often the crews would work 24-hour shifts. The noise was so loud that even with earplugs the men could hardly hear for hours after their shift.

The radar position at the Qawra Tower, photographed in 1943. These men are manning a listening device. The listening devices were designed to give early warning of the approach of an enemy aircraft. It is unclear whether this position was on the north-eastern coast of the Maltese mainland, close to St Paul's Bay, or at the Qawra Tower on the island of Gozo. In either case both structures were originally built by the Knights of St John in the seventeenth century. Qawra Tower near St Paul's Bay is now a restaurant and a swimming pool.

This is a Mark I transmitter and diesel, taken in 1941. Radar was in its infancy at this stage of the war and there were major problems with the transmitters overheating in the Maltese summer months. One of the lorries contained the transmitter, and a Meadows petrol engine generating set and a receiver were carried in a second lorry. There would also be two trailers to carry the telescopic wooden masts and aerials. The first site used on Malta was at Dingli, as at 817 feet (250m) it was the highest part of the island.

This is No. 3 gun, seen at Marsa. The anti-aircraft guns defending Malta included 3in (76mm), 3.7in (94mm) and 4.7in (120mm) pieces. The regiment in which Bill Lazell served, 7 HAA Regt, Royal Artillery, had twenty 3.7in guns and four 3in guns.

An often forgotten part of the anti-aircraft defence network across Malta was the Royal Malta Artillery. In 1938 it consisted of one regiment of three coastal batteries. During the Second World War it was greatly expanded. The 1st Coast Regiment consisted of four batteries; 2 Heavy Anti-Aircraft Regiment also had four batteries with one serving in Egypt; the 3 Light Anti-Aircraft Regiment had four batteries with one designated as the Dockyard Defence Battery, and 5 Coast Regiment and 11 Heavy Anti-Aircraft Regiment each had three batteries. Working alongside them was 8 Searchlight Battery, 4 Searchlight Regiment of the Royal Artillery and elements of 4 Heavy Anti-Aircraft Regiment, Royal Artillery.

This is No. 2 gun position at Marsa, seen at Easter 1942. Notice that the guns are not firing, due to a severe shortage of ammunition at that time. Although the gunners had been instructed to fire only at bombers, the enormous numbers of enemy aircraft overhead had meant that the number of shells fired was huge. It had been estimated that heavy anti-aircraft ammunition would have completely run out by the end of June 1942 and that even the light anti-aircraft guns would be without ammunition at the end of July. Governor Dobbie stated, 'If Malta is to be held, drastic action is needed now. It is a question of survival.'

This is another view of the larger anti-aircraft guns, also taken at Marsa. Notice that the gun is not firing despite the fact that bombers have clearly been overhead and have hit targets close by. The gunners were restricted to only a few rounds a day. In fact their daily amount could be fired off in a matter of minutes. As the raids petered out in summer 1942 the guns still had to be manned and the crews performed the same actions, including sighting, even though they had no ammunition to fire at the intruders.

A mobile anti-aircraft unit manoeuvres into position during an alert in 1941. Note the two-man crew in the rear have a tripod-mounted machine-gun and the driver has a Lee Enfield rifle secured beside him.

Obviously Malta's three airfields were the principal target of the formations of enemy aircraft, but also the industrial areas and harbours regularly came under attack. In April 1942 alone anti-aircraft gunners fired off over 160,000 rounds. Throughout the war around 30,000 of Malta's buildings were destroyed or badly damaged and around 1,100 civilians died in the bombings.

The island's defence depended very much on the close co-operation of the three branches of the armed forces, along with the Merchant Navy.

Chapter Three

The Blitz

When the word 'blitz' is used it is more often than not associated with London, but Malta's blitz lasted longer and in just two months in 1942 more bombs were dropped on Malta than fell on London throughout the war. London suffered fifty-seven days of continual raids; Malta suffered 154 days. Ta' Qali airfield was the most bombed allied airfield of the war. Every single village and town on the island was ruined even though the houses were made of vast limestone blocks. The Maltese and the garrison were forced to live in catacombs and underground shelters, their houses shattered. They had to hang their washing from trees, prepare their meals on the roads and sleep whenever they could between the raids. At the worst times four raids in a day meant ten to twenty hours of alerts and the alerts went on day after day, after day.

At times food was in short supply, as was water, as Malta does not have any fresh water reservoirs, lakes or rivers. Winter 1941 to 1942 was known as the Black Winter; there was hunger, lack of sleep, terror and destruction all around.

By the end of the blitz Malta would lie in ruins, the harbours and quaysides wrecked, the waters around the islands littered with sunken vessels. The countryside was scarred with craters and wrecked aircraft. Even when the longest siege was over, epidemics swept the island, claiming the weakened with tuberculosis and dysentery.

This unexploded German mine was buried in the earth. German aerial mines could weigh as much as 2,205lb (1,000kg) and have a charge weight of 1,500lb (680kg). In March 2008 the George Cross that was awarded to Brigadier Eastman was bought by the Queen's Royal Surrey Regiment Association. Eastman, along with Captain Jones, defused no less than 275 unexploded bombs on Malta in 1940.

This is 'Wacker' Coxon dealing with an unexploded German mine on Malta. Many tons of bombs were dropped on the Maltese islands during the Second World War. A large number of them failed to explode and many are still being found today. The German bombs usually failed due to the complex electric fuse mechanism, which was prone to failure. Perhaps the most famous enemy bomb can still be seen inside the St John's Co-Cathedral.

Peter Winstanley, who served with the 2nd Battalion, Royal Irish Fusiliers on Malta, recalled in 2005 a bizarre and terrifying incident regarding an unexploded Italian bomb. In the late summer of 1942 he was sitting in a NAAFI near the barracks at St George's Bay when a soldier came in somewhat drunk and carrying an Italian 500lb (227kg) bomb that he had found. He dumped it on the table and Peter and his companions had to wrestle the bomb from him, take it outside and throw it into the sea.

This Mark II receiver was at Marsa during the height of the blitz in 1942. This is a Mark II anti-aircraft gun-laying system, with a transmitter and receiver in separate trailer cabins. There were two 5in (13cm) display tubes, showing bearing and elevation. Security was very tight around these radar stations and it was the role of the Royal Electrical and Mechanical Engineers to put the stations together out of components made by several different factories.

A heavy barrage being put up by ground anti-aircraft units, as yet another German and Italian raid sweeps in over Malta. For two months in 1942 the only effective defence of Malta was the British anti-aircraft guns. During April German and Italian aircraft flew 10,323 sorties and dropped 7,000 tons of bombs. The anti-aircraft gunners claimed 102 kills, but the figure is probably closer to forty.

This is the No. 4 gun position at Marsa. During the critical period of 1942 German aircraft of Jagdgeschwader 53 braved the persistent and dangerous aerial defence over Malta. The anti-aircraft barrages were thick and it required nerve to ignore them while on a mission over the island. The anti-aircraft guns were controlled from the Operations Room in order to put up an umbrella of fire over Malta. The Italians called it 'The Gates of Hell'.

Germans pound positions on Malta, and in the foreground a watchtower built by the Knights of St John stands impassively. This unnamed tower could be the Ghajn Znuber Tower, on the north-east coast of Malta. According to the US Military Intelligence Services *Tactical and Technical Trends* (No. 6, August 27 1942):

The heavy and persistent air attacks on Malta have rightly earned for that small Mediterranean island the description 'the most bombed place on earth'. All heavy attacks were by day, with a few light raids by night. The Germans never employed straight, high level bombing. Full use was made of the sun and any available cloud cover. The practice of feinting was used – starting to dive towards one objective and then turning to attack the real target. The early attacks were by successive waves all approaching from the same direction and attacking the same objective. As the attack developed, the tactics varied, and synchronised attacks by waves of bombers approaching the same objective from different directions were common. The synchronisation became markedly better with practice. Alternatively, heavy attacks were made simultaneously on two targets, the object in either case being to confuse the defence. Later 'winners' would peel off from the main attack to make individual attacks on heavy anti-aircraft gun positions on the lines of approach or close to the target, or small formations would make deliberate diving attacks on gun positions, synchronising these attacks with the main attack. At least in the bombing attacks on Malta, Germans showed the trait, observed in the last war, of doing the same thing at the same time every day. During the heavy raids it was normal routine to receive an attack of about 75 bombers soon after breakfast, a second at lunch time, and a third at about 6 in the evening. This regularity was found to be a great convenience.

This considerable bomb damage was at Kingsway, Valletta, seen in 1942. This area of Valletta has a city gate known as Porta Reale, or 'Putirjal' in Maltese. The area suffered extensive damage during the Second World War. The main street of the city was originally known as Strada Reale, but it was changed to Kingsway as Italian understandably fell out of fashion.

A view of Spinola through barbed-wire defences. Spinola was one of Malta's main fishing villages and is near St George's Bay, on the north coast of the island. It was the regimental headquarters of 32 Light Anti-Aircraft Regiment. Houses were requisitioned, with officers living on the ground floors and other ranks upstairs. Beds were often blankets on stone floors and with no baths the sea was used with special saltwater soap.

This image of St John's Co-Cathedral was taken after an unwelcome visit from the Luftwaffe in 1942. The building was commissioned by the Grand Master of the Knights of St John and was completed between 1573 and 1578. The cathedral suffered severe damage and part of the annexe was virtually destroyed. The steeples were wrecked and the vestry was heavily damaged, with the main door being blown in.

Bomb damage in St Paul's Street, Valletta. Five years after the end of the war there was hardly a building in Valletta that did not show signs of bomb damage. Many parts of Valletta had to be evacuated during the heaviest of the bombing raids. Many of the citizens of Valletta who moved out during the war did not return and the population had dwindled to around 9,000 just after the war.

The Grand Harbour under attack, seen in 1941. Note that a crane has been hit and is falling into the water. When ships arrived in the Grand Harbour they had to be unloaded as quickly as possible, even during air raids. Between the raids the Grand Harbour returned to a sense of normality, with small ships weaving in and out of the shipwrecks and Maltese children playing along the quayside. Several ships were in fact hit in the harbour itself, such as HMS *Maori*, in February 1942. She was hit at her berth in the Grand Harbour and a bomb exploded in her engine room. Ammunition on board exploded and she settled by the stern. *Maori* was a Tribal Class destroyer.

Fires around the Grand Harbour, seen from Zebra Street in Birzebbugia. Birzebbugia was often referred to as 'Birsi' or 'Birzi' by the British garrison troops. The Italian and German plans to invade Malta had targeted Birzebbugia as a key objective, so that they could land supplies, heavy equipment and troops onto the island there. By day or night enemy bomber formations were escorted by large numbers of fighters. After a raid some of the fighters would peel off and attack British dispersal areas, gun positions, fishing boats or fighters that were about to land. The bombers were usually preceded by a fighter patrol and always followed by a reconnaissance patrol, operating at a higher altitude. After the bombers delivered their attacks they would take violent avoiding action. They would turn and change height until they were well clear of the islands. Normally, they did not come in low enough to make good enough targets for the light anti-aircraft guns and tended to leave these positions for the fighters once the main target had been struck.

St Publius's Church, in Floriana, close to Valletta. The church took a direct hit on 4 May 1941, wrecking the front door, glass windows and organ. One of the clocks still shows the time at which the bomb that hit the building struck: 09.40, yet the bells still continued to chime and the statue of the church's patron, St Publius, was safe, hidden in a niche behind an anti-blast wall and sandbags. At 07.50 on 28 April 1942 St Publius's Church was again hit by several bombs. The dome and roof collapsed onto the crypt, which was used as a public shelter, and under the weight of the fallen masonry thirteen people lost their lives.

An aerial view of the Mosta Dome. The dome is the third-largest unsupported dome in the world. On 9 April 1942 an enemy bomb hit the Mosta Dome; it went straight through without exploding. There were 300 people inside and none were injured. The incident took place at about 16.40, during a service. Incredibly the bomb bounced twice off the wall, and skidded the length of the nave and then came to a halt. The detonator of the bomb that fell in 1942 was removed and a replica of the bomb is displayed as a memorial. Unfortunately not everyone was so lucky that day, as an air-raid shelter at Luqa received a direct hit. It was destroyed, killing twenty-five people inside.

A raid on Ta' Qali by German Ju 87 Stukas in May 1942; the photograph was taken from the Zebbug gun position. By the middle of May 1942 a total of over 500 enemy aircraft had been claimed by the Maltese defenders and over fifty of them had been shot down in the first half of May alone. In April 1942 alone Ta' Qali received upwards of 400 tons of bombs in numerous attacks.

Bomb damage at Mile End, Valletta in 1942. Valletta is home to the Lascaris War Rooms, which were dug in the rock beneath Lascaris Bastion, near Barracca Gardens. They were part of an impregnable underground complex of rooms and passages that formed the nerve centre of Malta's defensive system during the Second World War. The war rooms were the venue for a meeting between General Dwight D Eisenhower, Allied Commander in Chief Mediterranean, Field Marshall Viscount Gort and Admiral of the Fleet Sir Andrew Cunningham. In a later statement Eisenhower said:

The epic of Malta is symbolic of the experience of the United Nations in this war. Malta has passed successively through the stages of woeful unpreparedness, tenacious endurance, intensive preparation, and the initiations of a fierce offensive. It is resolutely determined to maintain a rising crescendo of attack until the whole task is complete. For this inspiring example the United Nations will be forever indebted to Field Marshall Lord Gort, the fighting services under his command and to every citizen of the heroic island.

An aerial view of Malta, probably taken from a German photo-reconnaissance aircraft that was later shot down, and whose camera and film were later recovered. Note the promontory in the foreground of the island of Malta itself, with the Grand Harbour and other docks either side. In view to the rear of the photograph is Gozo.

Another aerial view, this time of the Grand Harbour, with Fort St Angelo in the centre. Valletta can be seen in the foreground. For many years Fort St Angelo was the only significant fortification on Malta, prior to the arrival of the Knights of St John in 1530. The British took over the fort in the nineteenth century, and in 1912 it became a naval shore establishment, listed as a ship, HMS *Egmont*. In 1933 it was renamed HMS *St Angelo*.

St Andrew's Barracks, near Sliema. This is a massive complex of messes, clubs, churches, gymnasiums and a cinema. It also incorporated a school and family accommodation. The barracks lies to the north-west of Sliema and many people from Valletta were evacuated there and spent two years crammed into the accommodation blocks, with up to twenty families to a barrack room. The family spaces were only separated by blankets on ropes. The large, white dining hall in the centre of the complex was used as a feeding station. Slip trenches were used as air-raid shelters, as were ground-floor storage bays. Conditions were ideal for the transfer of disease; enteric fever was rife. Civilians evacuated there swore that they could see Mount Etna on a clear day and also believed they could see German aircraft taking off from Sicily.

The dockyards on fire in the area around the Duke of York Avenue. This photograph was taken from Castile in spring 1942. Throughout March the Grand Harbour and the dockyards were under almost constant attack. Towards the end of March it seemed that the tempo of Luftwaffe attacks against Malta had increased. On 7 April the 2,000th alert was sounded, lasting for nearly twelve hours. The German action was affecting all areas of Maltese life; most of the bakeries had been put out of action, distribution centres for flour were destroyed and most homes had no power.

Flares and tracers over Luqa. Enemy aircraft would come in over the proposed target and drop parachute flares, in order for successive flights of bombers to be able to pinpoint their targets. It was primarily the role of Beaufighters to catch these Ju 88s and either shoot them down, scare them off or make them drop their flares prematurely. There was an altogether stranger but no less sinister object dropped on Christmas Day 1940. A sole Italian Fiat CR.42 buzzed over Malta on Christmas Day and dropped a small, metal cylinder. When it was opened it proved to be a Christmas greeting from a pilot of 72ª Squadriglia. It included a cartoon of a burly Italian pilot reaching out from his cockpit to attack British Hurricanes with his fists.

A barrage over the Grand Harbour. Note the use of flares, searchlights and tracers to both dissuade and detect incoming enemy aircraft. Bofors' tracers were a reddish pink, showing up well in the night sky. A Colour Sergeant of the Royal Marines, manning a battery on top of Fort St Angelo, described one raid on the Grand Harbour in January 1942:

The Sunday raids were interesting and exciting. We had two visits from Gerry. Bombs were dropped in and around the creeks, causing terrific clouds of dust, flying masonry and iron. Although I did not see it myself, it was stated that a motorcar complete went sailing over the top of us. The dust and spray often blinded our view, but the dive-bombers always came on. As they broke through the dust they seemed like hawks looking for prey. The sight was one never to be forgotten, the bursts of the heavies, the red tracers of the Bofors and light machine-guns, and the illumination made by the crashing planes all adding to the splendour of the day. Since these attacks I have witnessed many more dive bombing attacks from the same position and more concentrated on us. Although tragic, I must say it is very exciting and good sport to be having a crack at a dive-bomber. You lose all sense of fear and self preservation while it lasts.

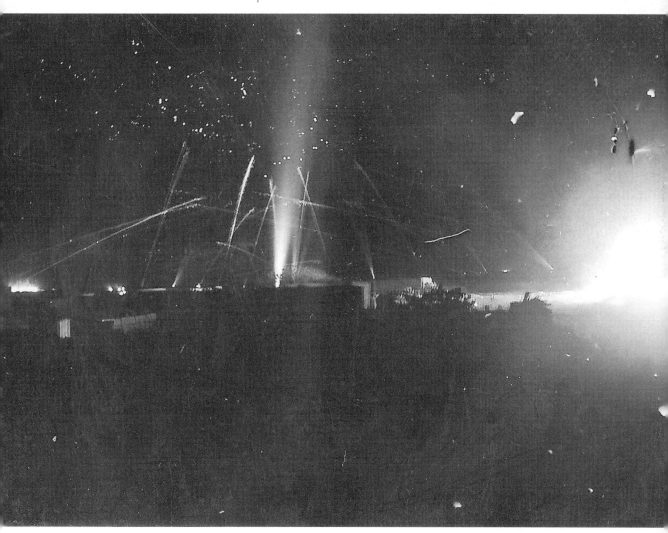

A German aerial view of Valletta. A great number of the aerial reconnaissance missions were in fact flown by Italians, particularly in the period up to 1942. For example, on 22 June 1940 a sole Savoia-Marchetti S79, flown by Tenente Francesco Solimena, approached the island. Group Captain George Burges recalled the incident:

'Timber' Woods [Flight Lieutenant William Woods DFC] and I were on the 16.00 hours to dusk watch when the alarm went off. We took off and climbed as hard as we could go, as was the custom. We did not attempt to maintain close formation because if one aircraft could climb faster than the other, then the additional height gained might be an advantage. Ground control as usual gave us the position and course of the enemy. The enemy turned out to be a single SM79 presumably on a photographic sortie. 'Timber' went in first but I did not see any result. I managed to get right behind it and shot off the port engine. The aircraft caught fire and crashed in the sea off Kalafrana.

The Maltese Police Fire Service, hard at work in Valletta after an enemy air attack. As many of the buildings were made of limestone, effectively a large block of rock, fire was not so much of a problem as in other towns and cities across Europe. But there were still rescues to be made and rubble to be cleared. Sirens were installed at police stations and at ARP centres. During air raids where there was a lack of shelters civilians would hide under their dining tables and once the all-clear had been called they would scan the skies for an Italian reconnaissance plane, which would signal another imminent attack.

Marsa during a particularly heavy bombardment in 1942. Here two servicemen have taken shelter and can only watch as the enemy aircraft do their worst. Many of the air-raid shelters, both permanent and ad hoc, took advantage of the sturdy limestone buildings around the Maltese countryside. Many servicemen had close calls; pilots and crew of No. 601 Squadron on an evening off were in Valletta and were heading for the Mayfair Hotel when they heard bombers overhead. They found themselves amidst an avalanche of masonry. Nonetheless they searched for a bar and tried to enjoy their short break from duties.

The Royal Opera House after being hit in April 1942. It was considered to be the finest building in Valletta. There has been considerable debate about the future of the Royal Opera House site. It was cleared of most of the rubble and rebuilding programmes were repeatedly postponed or cancelled. In the 1950s a number of architects submitted designs for a new theatre, but by the end of the decade the project had been shelved. Still successive Maltese governments refuse to make a concrete decision about what remains of the magnificent building. It is used as an open-air performance venue. The original structure was designed by Edward Middleton Barry, who also designed the Royal Opera House in Covent Garden and numerous grand buildings around Britain. The building was completed in 1866, but later some of its interior was gutted by a fire.

A view of Kingsway, Valletta after a bombing attack. Kingsway is now known as Republic Street. Valletta was named a World Heritage site by UNESCO in 1980. One of the popular venues on Kingsway was the Casino Maltese. Many of its customers were servicemen during the war, and unfortunately, on 15 February 1942, it was hit in an air raid and several members of staff lost their lives. The building was originally the treasury of the Knights of St John.

The ruins of the Capitol Cinema in Valletta in 1941. The cinema was located on St John's Street. All of the other cinemas of the period are now closed down, including the Savoy, Embassy, Coliseum and Imperial. Some have been converted, whereas others, having suffered damage during the war, have been demolished and replaced with more modern buildings. A shopping mall occupies the site of the former Capitol Cinema.

More bomb damage on Kingsway. Kingsway stretched the length of Valletta, from Kingsgate to Fort St Elmo, and in effect was the main street of the city. In the picture The New House is marked 'D Portelli'. This may relate to Casa Caccia, which was let to Sir Agostino Portelli, the first president of the Malta Chamber of Commerce, in 1839. The building was totally destroyed by a German parachute mine.

Chapter Four

The Maltese and the Garrison

The garrison and the British civilians on Malta found the island and the people to be friendly. The Maltese have a close-knit culture, with many of the families linked together by marriage. The garrison was more likely to mix with the Maltese civilians rather than with the British civilians because, like many British abroad in difficult or near-impossible circumstances they drew together and became very insular. Clearly there would have been times when there were tensions between the garrison forces and the Maltese, but the object of Maltese scorn and hatred was the Italians. These close neighbours were not forgiven for bombing Malta, for destroying homes and for being responsible for bellies being empty, not to mention the interrupted sleep.

There were some levels of resentment because the Maltese often acted with great gallantry and selflessness, yet despite this they were ignored or overlooked while, they believed, the British servicemen's actions were glorified. A common phrase was, 'If a Britisher sneezes, he gets a medal for it.' Typical of the Maltese servicemen operating anti-aircraft guns during the German and Italian attacks was a man who was hit between the shoulders by a shell splinter. He remained at his post even though he was in excruciating pain and could not move his neck. He received no reward or praise for his act, yet a British warrant officer was awarded the MBE for diving into a bombed-out kitchen to retrieve pots and pans so his men could eat.

The Maltese faced the ordeal in the best way they could and every effort was made, particularly by Gort, to try to make sure that relations between the garrison and the townspeople and villagers remained cordial. There were some who believed that elements of the Maltese population, including the Bishop of Gozo, were anti-British, but in the end these suspicions were unfounded, as the Bishop of Gozo was prominent at the George Cross award ceremony and later pleaded with the British authorities for a repeat ceremony to be held on Gozo itself.

Relations between British servicemen and Maltese girls were problematic. Many of them were chaperoned if they were allowed to date a serviceman. It was estimated that around 2,000 Maltese girls were attached to Royal Navy men at some point and most of these were abandoned when the Royal Navy moved on to new theatres of war.

Siggiewi, in the south-west of Malta, is three miles (5km) from Mdina and about six miles (10km) to the west of Valletta. The centre of rural Siggiewi is dominated by the baroque parish church of St Nicholas. Second-World-War structures still remain in Siggiewi, and the town boasts what is claimed to be the best-preserved example of a Second-World-War military airstrip on Malta. The airfield was used as a Second-World-War decoy to lure German bombers away from Luqa airport and it also played an important part in British plans to liberate Sicily. Qrendi-based Spitfires would escort bombers and transport aircraft to support the allied troops in Sicily, and they were also used in bombing sorties. An enormous number of people from Valletta were evacuated to Siggiewi and in fact the population grew by more than 5,000, trebling its pre-war population.

Members of 7 HAA Regt, Royal Artillery: including Steve ?, Pete Holdy, Ron Wills, Frank Jeff, Eddie Dainty, Bill Harvey, Scotty, 'Busty' Hipwood, Mick Roy, Jack Milne, Binny Barnes, Dougy Marcort, Tommy Giles, ? Goodwin, and Ossie Chambers. Bill Lazell is pictured in the bottom left of the picture, with the Lewis gun across his lap. Many of the men arrived on Malta in July 1941 and remained on the island, operating radar and heavy anti-aircraft guns until their departure in March 1944.

This shows Ken Barker of the Royal Artillery, at Lancer GL position in 1943, offering chocolate to local Maltese women. Some canny Maltese dug holes in their back gardens and lined them with tarpaulin. Inside they secreted tinned food, matches and kerosene and then buried their treasure, even covering up the spot with shrubs and plants. It became illegal for people to have large stocks of imported goods, and government inspectors would routinely check homes.

The men of 7 HAA Regt, Royal Artillery, were billeted in Siggiewi, in this former stable, in March 1942 and were often accompanied at night by a donkey. The families in Siggiewi took in complete strangers who had fled from Valletta and Senglea during heavy bombing raids, which devastated most of the cities and caused many deaths. The entire cities and neighbouring areas had to be evacuated. On 20 June 1943 King George VI visited Senglea and praised the gallantry of its citizens.

This shot shows members of the Royal Artillery anti-aircraft battery at Marsa in 1942 unloading ammunition, a dangerous and unwelcome fatigue duty. Marsa was always at the forefront of bombing raids during the Second World War. Anti-aircraft positions were placed on Jesuits' Hill, which served as a fortress. At many times throughout the siege of Malta ammunition was at a premium.

A Royal Artilleryman taking a well-earned rest at the Siggiewi No. 2 position. Note the dual-purpose camouflage and sunshade and the near-prehistoric seating arrangements. It was impractical for the gun crews to even try to return to their billets during their breaks due to the unpredictable pattern of the enemy attacks and the fact that transport was at a premium. Invariably there was no electricity or water.

A Maltese farmer's cowshed, which was used as a billet. Maltese farms, like many farms in Mediterranean countries, are relatively small and as far as livestock are concerned concentrate on cattle, pigs, sheep, goats and chicken. Most of the vegetable cash crops are potatoes, melons, onions and tomatoes. Vine growing remains an important part of farming activity on Malta.

Members of 7 HAA Regt, Royal Artillery. Anti-aircraft units would do two months of day shifts followed by a month of nights. The high points were the social evenings in the NAAFI halls, usually held on a Monday. Sometimes there would be cinema shows and concert parties and pantomimes. Efforts were always being made to keep morale as high as possible.

The Royal Artillerymen taking a break. Most of the men spent 24 hours, 7 days a week at or around their posts. If they were lucky they would get two or three days off a month. Buses were extremely irregular due to the petrol crisis, but it was always possible to borrow a bicycle. Keeping billets clean and presentable was important, as was ensuring that the uniforms were kept tidy and army discipline demanded that belts and buttons remained polished, even though men found it difficult to find polish, and detergent to wash their clothes.

This is the Verdala position on 28 January 1944. From right to left, Bill Lazell, 'Wacker' Coxon, Ken Barker, Les ? and Pete Holdy. This picture was taken just a few weeks before Bill Lazell's regiment left Malta in March 1944. Kit inspections were still important to maintain discipline and a sense of pride. It was an offence to become sunburned, and anti-aircraft crews would keep their shirts on and their sleeves rolled down. It had taken time to acclimatise to the local weather. Drinking was an important pastime; mosquitoes were a constant irritation and the dreaded Malta dog, or dysentery, was a threat that could easily have thinned the ranks even more.

Men of 7 HAA Regt, Royal Artillery, with Bill Lazell on the far right of the centre row. At the end of the 24-hour shift the men would be exhausted. Even when they were off duty they would find it impossible to sleep due to being billeted so close to their positions, listening to the crashes of bombs and the sound of anti-aircraft guns firing. The men were often infested with fleas and would scratch themselves raw. The high point of the day would be heating up tins of Maconachie's pies and bully beef. When the men first arrived in 1941 they would think of nothing of walking into Valletta on their days off, but as the war progressed, with many of the cinemas and bars closed or destroyed there was far less interest in doing this to break the monotony.

Enterprising young Maltese boys selling prickly pears along Mile End in Valletta. Prickly pears, also known as cactus figs, were tricky to eat but delicious and they also formed the basis of the Bajtra liqueur. The prickly pear was introduced to the Mediterranean at the end of the fifteenth century from the Americas. It flourishes in the rubble-walled countryside and is often used as a boundary plant. The fruit is collected in August and September.

The Barracca lift. The lift connected the upper Barracca Gardens with Lascaris Wharf. It was used by people who wanted to get to the middle of Valletta from the wharf without having to climb the steep streets. It was also well known as Malta's lovers' leap. At the time of writing the lift is not in operation, although there are plans to reopen it. Many claimed that the lift itself was constructed out of old bed frames and was something of a perilous ride.

Navy personnel on leave in Strait Street, a popular destination for servicemen in Valletta, as it was the centre for uniform outfitters and tattoo parlours. Malta was a favoured stopping-off point for the Royal Navy. The White Ensign and the Vernon clubs were close to the jetty at the Grand Harbour. The Gut was also a popular narrow alleyway full of bars, restaurants, dance halls and was also Valletta's red-light district.

Maltese farm girls at work near St Paul's Bay. Terrace farming is used a great deal on Malta. Traditionally Malta would import more food than it exported and was not self-sufficient. In order to try to deal with the shortfall in food during the Second World War and to increase production cauliflowers, onions, potatoes, tomatoes and wheat were all grown in greater quantities, but the crops were still small due to the rocky soil. Maltese soil has little in the way of nutrients, contributing to the poor harvests.

Quarrying stone at Fort Manoel in Valletta. The fortification, built by the Knights of St John, was constructed between 1723 and 1755. It stands on Manoel Island, commanding the entrance to Marsamxett Harbour and Sliema Creek. There was a battery of 3.7in (94mm) heavy anti-aircraft guns deployed in and around the fort during the Second World War. The guns were mounted in concrete emplacements in a semicircle around the fort.

Fresh water being poured into a horse-drawn barrel or keg. Owing to the bombing water supplies were at best haphazard. People would queue up for water, fuel and bread. People were reduced to using their own furniture as fuel, either to keep warm or to cook a hot meal. Bread was in very short supply and staples like pasta, rice and tomato paste were heavily rationed. The livestock had to be culled, particularly the pigs, sheep and goats; there was simply no fodder for them. Horses such as this, however, were spared as they were needed for transportation.

A traditional Maltese horse-drawn bus outside the Castile in 1942. The smaller, traditional horse-drawn carriage of Malta, the Karozzin, survives to this day. It dates back to the nineteenth century and is still appreciated for its heritage quality. During the war Karrozins and larger horse-drawn omnibuses became a vital link between the villages.

Shelters and dwellings at Cospicua, which was one of the so-called Three Cities, along with Vittoriosa and Senglea. In 1940, 40 per cent of the combined population of the Three Cities and those of Valletta, Floriana and Sliema, lived in the inner harbour area, and 94 per cent of Malta's entire population lived within 14.5 square miles of all of the urban areas. When Italy entered the war Cospicua had a population of 13,000. Many stayed put initially despite the fact that they had been advised to evacuate. After the start of the air raids many did evacuate, taking with them just their essential belongings loaded onto prams, buses, touring cars, cabs and horse-drawn vehicles. On 14 June 1940 a wave of twenty-five aircraft came in over Cospicua. It was badly hit and casualties were heavy. Those who had not evacuated now began to reconsider. Nonetheless, throughout the siege the church bells in Cospicua continued to ring, if nothing else but to proclaim a grim determination to survive.

The market in Strada Mercanti, Valletta. Many of the commercial buildings of Valletta were found in Strada San Giorgio, Strada Mercanti, Strada Forni and Strada San Paolo. There were also a great number of residential buildings, with shops and a handful of public buildings. Even in the centre of Valletta fresh goats' milk was sold door-to-door by the simple expedient of bringing goats down the street. It was discovered in 1905 that the unpasteurised goats' milk was the cause behind the undulant fever, or Mediterranean fever, a disease that threatened to become an epidemic. The large wrecked building is the marketplace, a large roofed structure, where almost anything was bought and sold.

Horse-drawn oil sellers at Pawla, which is to the south of Valletta and was founded in 1826 by the Knights of St John. There were shortages in almost every commodity, and oil was no exception. While the garrison focused on the need for flour, oil, fuel, ammunition and aircraft spares, the Maltese people scratched around for cloth and leather, and were often forced to tear down their curtains to make a dress or a pair of trousers. Parachute silk was a much-welcomed commodity. People used rubber from old car tyres to replace worn-out shoe soles. As soon as the all-clear had been sounded people would queue for oil, as they used kerosene for cooking. By June 1942 kerosene had run out entirely and this was yet another blow to the thousands who had been made homeless or been forced to abandon their properties. Poor living conditions and insufficient food made everyone prone to disease.

Maltese families evacuating from Senglea. One of the early plans was to evacuate areas thought to be at risk. Senglea, with a population of 8,000, was one of these. Families seemed to believe that the centre of the island would be the safest place. In a matter of days the towns and their squares and streets close to the harbour and to the coast were abandoned, all barring hundreds of hungry animals. By early August 1940 the official estimate was that there were over 81,000 refugees; around a quarter of the population. Many were billeted in Birkirkara, Qormi, Rabat, Mosta, Zejtun, Zebbug, Safi and Lija. The governor had announced on 15 June that each village would have an official, later given the title of Protection Officer. They would work with the District Committee, the police and the special constabulary to deal with refugees and ensure they had food and accommodation.

This photograph shows the aftermath of sabotage in the Grand Harbour in January 1943. At the outbreak of the war pro-Italian Maltese accounted for as many as one in five of the population. Some Italian Maltese wanted to actually unify with Italy and some joined the Italian military during the war. One such pro-Italian Maltese national, Carmelo Borg Pisani, was executed at Corradino Prison on Malta on 28 November 1942. He had been sent on a secret mission by the Italians but from the outset it was a disaster and, trapped in a sea cave, he called for help to a British patrol boat. He was arrested, interrogated and charged with treason. Around seventeen Maltese were also accused on charges of treason, although none of the others were given the death penalty.

The Carlton Cinema, in Sliema, showing *Bulldog Drummond's Peril*. Note also the advertising posters for *The Mikado*, *Marie Antoinette* and Charles Laughton in *Jamaica Inn*. The cinema itself dates from the 1920s and after the Second World War it was gutted and became a Marks and Spencer store. *Bulldog Drummond's Peril* was released in 1938. The character was originally created by Herman Cyril McNeile. *Jamaica Inn* was an Alfred Hitchcock 1939 movie adaptation of Daphne du Maurier's book, set in Cornwall around 1800. *The Mikado* was a landmark film, as it featured a complete Gilbert and Sullivan Savoy operetta filmed in Technicolor.

Before the blitz, a pleasant Sunday morning ride in Birkirkara. The statue of Maria Bambina was taken from the Church of Senglea to Birkirkara for safekeeping and on 24 January 1941 the statue of the Immaculate Conception was also taken there. On 19 November 1944 the statue was finally taken back to its home in Cospicua. Birkirkara became a very important refugee centre during the Second World War.

A farming family at work in Siggiewi. During summer 1942 food stocks diminished severely; bread was being made with 20 per cent potatoes and most adults barely received 1,000 calories a day. The bread ration was slashed to 300g (10oz) per person per day on 5 May 1942. Communal victory kitchens were established and at their peak there were 200 of these; in October 1942 they were catering for 100,000 people daily. By January 1943 more than 175,000 people were being fed via the kitchens. The staple diet for most people was goats' meat in tomato sauce with beans. Minced goat meat was even turned into loaves of bread, and the stalks and skin of vegetables were left intact just to eke out a meal. Rations for the troops were no more generous. Everyone was always hungry, they drank heavily chlorinated water, there was no butter, cheese, eggs or milk, and meals would consist of Chinese pilchards, corned beef and dry biscuits. Sometimes they would fry up bully beef and add in biscuits and pilchards, just to change the texture of what they were eating. Servicemen who had weighed 70 or 80kg (11 or 12 stone) were now down to 50kg (8st). Starvation was a definite danger and no one ever dared to talk about food.

Another farm scene. Supplementing rations with the odd treat was always a preoccupation for the garrison. This meant maintaining good relations with local farmers, as this was the key to success. Foodstuffs were so scarce that even locally grown vegetables were in short supply. Parents would pretend that they were not hungry so that their children could eat. Prized possessions for civilians were tins of bacon, ship's biscuits and bars of chocolate. Children would steal one another's lunchboxes and understandably they would often cry with hunger. By the time the war was over, many of them were suffering from malnutrition. There was no winter clothing left in the shops and there was brisk bartering between servicemen and civilians for army blankets to make coats and jackets. Sandals were made from rope and bits of heavy cotton.

An army truck in the Maltese countryside. Note the unusual camouflage scheme used. The truck, including the tarpaulin, has been painted to resemble traditional Maltese limestone walling. From a distance or from the air the truck would have been virtually invisible. Enemy aircraft would focus on key targets, but German fighters in particular would hunt for targets of opportunity. This meant that any part of the countryside was potentially dangerous. Children were told to make sure that they touched nothing while they were playing. Anti-personnel mines were dropped that looked like pens or cans of sardines. Many children were badly injured. Bomb sites were a draw to them and they were under constant danger from falling shells, shrapnel and other hazards like unstable buildings. One child exploring a bomb site at the Point du Vue Hotel in Rabat entered what was left of a building and found the bodies of five decapitated servicemen.

Chapter Five

Convoys and Hope

On 10 January 1941 HMS *Illustrious* steamed into the Grand Harbour at the head of a convoy. She had been attacked for seven hours by German dive-bombers, and for the duration of her stay in Valletta she remained under almost constant attack.

The convoys, whether carrying food, reinforcements, spares, ammunition or new aircraft, were a lifeline for Malta throughout the siege.

In May 1941 HMS *Eagle* and USS *Wasp* began their deliveries of Spitfires to Malta. Convoys would have to run the gauntlet from either Gibraltar or Alexandria to get to Malta. Even when they had arrived they were not safe and smokescreens were put up by portable smoke canisters in the Grand Harbour.

The most significant convoy was codenamed Operation Pedestal or, as the Maltese called it, The Santa Marija Convoy, as it was due to arrive on 13 August 1942, two days before the feast day of the ascension of the Virgin Mary. It left Gibraltar on 10 August and came under frenzied attack from the Italians and the Germans. By 12 August, with the covering escort, Force Z, having turned back to Gibraltar, the convoy faced the last and most dangerous thirty-six hours. After coming under attack from German U-boats and Italian submarines, as well as aircraft, the main body of the convoy finally reached the Grand Harbour. Others would struggle in later. Nine vessels had been lost or forced to turn back. For the Maltese and the garrison it was a much-needed morale boost. For many, Operation Pedestal was not the end, but the beginning of the end of the siege.

The most precious merchant ship to arrive in August 1942 was USS *Ohio*. She had been hit *en route*, and the British had tried to tow her but failed and she was still under attack by enemy aircraft. By the afternoon of 13 August *Ohio* had sixteen Spitfires protecting her at all times. As a result the enemy only managed to hit her once, but still she would not sink. By the evening the enemy had virtually given up their convoy attack and had switched their attention to the ships that were limping back to Gibraltar. HMS *Bramham* had picked up the survivors of *Dorset* and could not find any sign of *Manchester*. She now returned to help *Ohio* in.

A dangerous and novel plan was brought together to get *Ohio* into port. HMS *Bramham* was tied to one side and HMS *Penn* to the other. Slowly the ships began to inch towards the Grand Harbour. It took them until 08.00 on 15 August to finally get into the Grand Harbour, by which time a band was waiting for them and the bastions of Valletta were heaving with crowds waving and cheering.

In all some 55,000 tons of supplies had been delivered. Nine of the fourteen merchantmen that had been sent out had been lost along with four Royal Navy vessels. But Malta now had sufficient fuel. The arrival of *Ohio* coincided with an important feast day on Malta – Santa Marija (Saint Mary). The arrival of the fuel and the food brought both real and symbolic hope to the islanders and defenders. It would not be the last convoy, but certainly one of the most dramatic.

A convoy heading for Malta, under aerial attack. Planning for Operation Pedestal had begun in mid-July 1942. It was to be the largest ever convoy bound for Malta and also the most heavily escorted. The main problem was to find merchant ships that could maintain a reasonable speed despite the fact that there had been enormous merchant shipping losses in the North Atlantic and in the Mediterranean. The merchant ships would have to travel at 15 knots (22mph). Twelve vessels were chosen, each of which would be given the same basic load of fuel, food, ammunition, mechanical spares and medical supplies. This meant that even if most of the ships did not get through, the island would receive a delivery of each of the vital supplies. The Admiralty also knew that even if all of the ships got through it would never be enough, but it would mean a great deal to Malta.

The Royal Navy protecting merchant ships *en route* to Malta. When Operation Pedestal sailed past Gibraltar and into the Mediterranean on the night of 9 to 10 August 1942 they slowed down to allow the destroyers to steam into Gibraltar for refuelling. The convoy was spotted by an Italian spy in Spanish Morocco. It would now have to run the gauntlet of 650 enemy aircraft, six cruisers, nineteen E-boats, sixteen submarines and five destroyers. The first attack came in just after lunch on 11 August, when HMS *Eagle*, an aircraft carrier, sank in minutes to the south of the Balearic Islands, having been hit by four torpedoes fired by a German U-boat.

A convoy at anchor off Malta, having safely run the gauntlet from Gibraltar. Operation Pedestal came under enormous pressure once they were to the south of Sardinia on 12 August 1942. A Ju 88 hit the merchant vessel *Deucalion*, disabling her. Her crew was picked up, but persistence managed to get her back underway at 8 knots (12mph). The German aircraft arrived later in the day to try and finish her off. A pair of Heinkel bombers fired torpedoes at her and this time the merchant ship's charmed life (this was her second voyage to Malta) was over; she exploded and sank.

An impressive array of ships off the coast of Malta, this photograph was presumably taken in the aftermath of the siege and in the build-up to Operation Husky, the invasion of Sicily. Operation Husky was launched on 10 July 1943 and it was from Malta that General Dwight D Eisenhower sailed to take his first step on enemy-held Europe, just two days later. Each and every enemy aircraft that dared venture anywhere near Malta in the closing weeks was swatted from the skies for fear that they would spot the preparations. From this point onwards, Malta became a strike base and every single enemy aircraft destroyed in the air or on the ground brought prospects of the invasion's success closer. Malta's Spitfires were making daily sweeps over Sicily and beyond.

A Malta convoy under attack. While *Deucalion* was being lost the rest of Operation Pedestal's convoy also came under attack. HMS *Indomitable* took three hits from German bombers and part of the deck collapsed, HMS *Cairo* and HMS *Nigeria* were both hit by torpedoes, the oil tanker *Ohio* was also hit by a torpedo, but now the convoy had reached a point where Force Z, the heavy escort including the aircraft carriers, had to turn back towards Gibraltar. Now there was no allied air cover and Force X was now moving to try to protect the convoy.

Eagerly awaiting the arrival of convoy ships in Valletta. It was a ruse that had saved the remnants of the vessels of Operation Pedestal. They had been under almost constant attack from Ju 87s and Ju 88s, but now the RAF, knowing that the Italians were listening to radio traffic, pretended to talk in a Liberator bomber strike against Italian surface vessels. The Italians fell for the ruse at 02.00 on 13 August and turned away. The merchantmen and their escorts could now steam on towards Malta. Soon they would be in range of Spitfire cover and at early light on 13 August Spitfires were sent out to find them.

This photograph shows Royal Artillerymen being ferried into Malta in 1941 from Alexandria, onboard HMS *Manxman*. HMS *Manxman* was commissioned on 20 June 1941 and was a Abdiel Class fast minelayer. In August 1941 she carried reinforcements and supplies from Gibraltar to Malta and in November 1942 she made a similar voyage from Alexandria to Malta. She was torpedoed and badly damaged by the German submarine *U-375*, off Algeria, on 1 December 1942. Subsequently repairs would take until April 1945, after which time she joined the Pacific Fleet and arrived at Melbourne at the beginning of August 1945. In June 1957 she was mothballed at Malta until she underwent a refit at Gibraltar between 1958 and 1960. After being used in Borneo and Singapore, she was finally broken up in 1971. Her ship's bell is in the War Museum at Valletta.

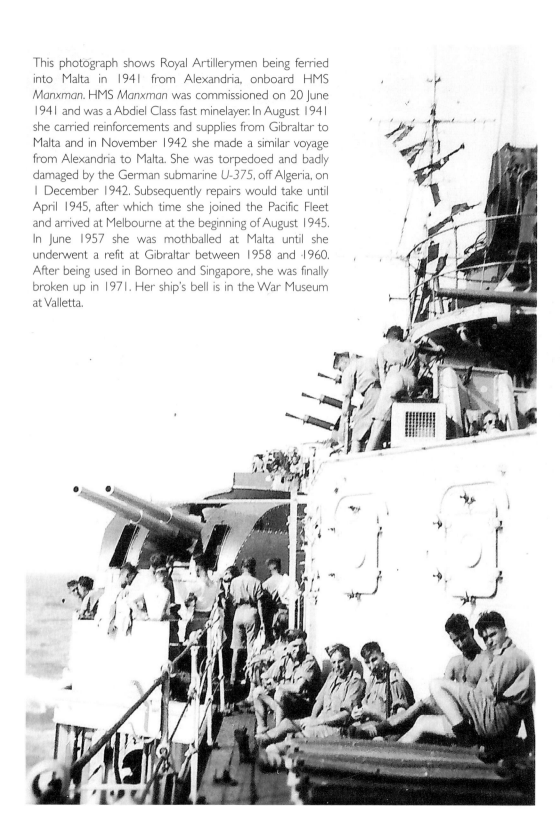

HMS *Upholder* off the Maltese coast, possibly in 1941. She was a Unity Class submarine built originally for training surface ships in anti-submarine detection, but because they could dive so quickly they were ideal for the Mediterranean. The Commanding Officer, Lieutenant Commander Wanklyn, reached Marsamxett Harbour after a month's journey at the beginning of January 1941. HMS *Upholder* would become one of the most successful submarines operating in the Mediterranean. They completed twenty-four patrols and sank around 120,000 tons of enemy shipping, including a destroyer, a cruiser, three U-boats, three troop transports, two tankers, a trawler and ten cargo ships. *Upholder* was attached to the 10th Submarine Flotilla, based on Malta. Unfortunately she was lost with all hands on her twenty-fifth patrol. She had been sent to intercept a convoy on 6 April 1942. She fell victim to depth charges off the North African coast, probably on 14 April. Other suggestions are that she was sunk when she struck a mine close to Tripoli on 11 April.

The arrival of MV *Melbourne Star* in the Grand Harbour on 13 August 1942 as part of the Operation Pedestal effort to bring supplies to Malta. She was launched in 1936 and was part of the Blue Star Line. She saw her first act of war in November 1940 when she was attacked by a German aircraft to the west of the Republic of Ireland. She was again attacked *en route* to Malta on 24 July 1941, but managed to arrive safely in Valletta. Unfortunately *Melbourne Star* did not survive the war. On 2 April 1943, to the south-east of Bermuda, she was torpedoed by the German submarine *U-129*. She was bound for Panama and Australia out of Liverpool and went down with a mixed load, including torpedoes and ammunition. Only four of her crew of seventy-five survived, along with eleven gunners and thirty-one passengers.

Another shot of *Melbourne Star* as she reaches the safety of the Grand Harbour. Of the merchant ships that managed to make it through to Malta, *Melbourne Star* arrived, along with *Port Chalmers* and *Rochester Castle* on 13 August. The following day, damaged, *Brisbane Star* arrived. She was the sister ship of *Melbourne Star*. *Brisbane Star* had been hit by a German aircraft torpedo off Skuki Channel on 12 August, but fortunately only one crewmember had been lost. *Ohio* arrived on 15 August.

An unidentified major British surface vessel, probably a Nelson Class battleship, either HMS *Rodney* or HMS *Nelson*. Both of these vessels were part of Force H, which operated in the Mediterranean, performing escort duties for convoys running into Malta. These monstrous battleships were launched in 1925 and commissioned five years later. HMS *Rodney* had been involved in the hunt for the Germans' last battleship, *Bismarck*. *Rodney* would later be involved in Operations Torch, Husky and Overlord. She steamed nearly 160,000 nautical miles during the course of the war but was finally sold for scrap in 1948. HMS *Nelson* survived for just a year longer but not before she had suffered the indignity of being a target vessel for bombing exercises.

This is a captured Italian E-boat, moored in the Grand Harbour. Italian E-boats were extremely fast and potent weapons. In July 1941 the Italians had launched an audacious attack on the Grand Harbour using E-boats. On the night of 26 July a number of these light Italian motor launches attempted to steal into the Grand Harbour and Marsamxett to destroy a newly arrived convoy as it was being unloaded. The Italians were trying to repeat a successful mission that they had launched against HMS *York* in Souda Bay, Crete, in March 1941 when they had crippled the cruiser. But this time they were quickly spotted and in fact they had been detected by Hurricane night-fighters as they approached the Grand Harbour. The Italian launches were pinpointed by searchlights and pummelled with anti-aircraft guns, machine-guns and 6pdr artillery shells. In six minutes the Italians were wiped out. They would later claim that the massacre of their sneak attack was a 'monstrous atrocity'.

The RAF Air-Sea Rescue Service also operated out of Malta, but at Kalafrana. In summer 1941 the only ASR cover was HSL107. Between 1940 and 1944 she picked up sixty-seven allied aircrew and sixteen Italians and Germans. On Malta ASR was something of a make-do affair and seaplane tenders were also used. As more RAF fighters were transferred to Malta, ASR cover became more important and in July 1941 three launches were due to be delivered from Gibraltar. Two of the launches got through in the October. Despite this the ASR on Malta used three seaplane tenders and twelve other craft of various types throughout the siege.

More convoy vessels lay off the Maltese coast. Almost certainly this shot would have been taken towards the end of 1943, where the prospect of enemy air attack or danger from submarines had receded to the extent that the vessels would not need the protection of the harbour.

Operation Husky itself was an enormous undertaking. 160,000 allied troops, 14,000 vehicles, 600 tanks and 1,800 guns were deployed against an enemy force believed to be in excess of 300,000. Until the very last minute the Germans mistakenly believed that the allied troops amassing would actually strike against Greece, due to a deception plan codenamed Operation Mincemeat, in which documents were attached to a corpse that had been allowed to wash up on a beach in Spain.

Chapter Six

Victory and Celebrations

The final air raids on Malta came on 26 February 1943 when Italians attempted some hit-and-run attacks, but they were beaten off. For Malta this was a landmark day. Throughout the siege 547 British aircraft had been lost in air combat and another 160 on the ground. The Germans and Italians had lost 1,252 aircraft over the island and in addition there were 1,052 probable kills. It had not just been the RAF that had fended off the aerial invaders; notable contributions were made by the anti-aircraft guns, Fleet Air Arm and Royal Navy vessels.

By 1944 Malta had adopted a new role as a bridgehead between North Africa and the European mainland. It was now an armed camp and the island was like a massive aircraft carrier, with enormous offensive capacity.

Understandably, both the garrison and the locals on Malta were not only relieved but also delighted that the epic of Malta was now over. No more would the skies over Valletta be filled with enemy aircraft intent on destruction. The celebrations, both formal and informal, swept across the island. Malta had experienced 3,349 air-raid alerts, with the last alert being sounded on 28 August 1944. Each village and town on the island was scarred and disfigured and for years memories of the blitz remained; to this day the Opera House lies in ruins, the only landmark that has not been rebuilt.

There were some who had said that if the British had surrendered at Malta, as they did at Singapore against the Japanese, the Maltese people would have suffered less during the siege. Malta was granted independence in September 1964. For ten years the island retained the British monarch as its queen, with a Governor General. In 1974 it became a republic. Five years later British military forces withdrew from Malta for the last time.

A picture of the Gloster Gladiator *Faith*, faithfully part-restored. In September 1943 *Faith*, one of the original Gladiators that had faced the Italians three years before, was retrieved from the bottom of the quarry in which she had lain. She was presented to the people of Malta by Air Marshall Sir Keith Park. *Faith* very much represented the courage and the fortitude of the servicemen and the civilians of Malta. *Faith* is, perhaps, the best-known of the three and she was fitted with an engine that was salvaged from a Bristol Blenheim. She also had a three-bladed propeller, rather than the standard two blades. *Charity* was shot down on 29 July 1940 and *Hope* was destroyed in an air raid on 4 February 1941. The fuselage of *Faith*, as seen in the picture, is now on display at the Malta War Museum in Fort St Elmo in Valletta. In recent years there has been considerable public pressure to move *Faith* from the war museum to the Malta Aviation Museum Foundation, where the intention would be to rebuild her so that she could be restored to her former glory. The feeling is that she should be seen alongside examples of the Spitfire and the Hurricane, the three aircraft that personify the fighting spirit of Malta, even in the darkest days.

Another shot of *Faith* at the official handing-over ceremony in Valletta. The quarry to which *Faith* had been consigned was alongside the Hal Far road, directly behind the RAF Officers' Mess building and probably 137 Maintenance Unit. The quarries were used to dump aircraft that had been shot down after they had been stripped of useful parts. Very little has actually been done to the remnants of *Faith* since 1974, when the RAF put a fresh skin on the fuselage and painted her in wartime colours.

Another shot of *Faith*. The Gloster Gladiator was the last biplane used by the RAF, but it was also the first that had a fully enclosed cockpit. By September 1939 there were large numbers of Gloster Gladiators being used around the Mediterranean and the Middle East. The original three Gloster Gladiators were initially four that had been packed in crates and left at the flying-boat base at Kalafrana when HMS *Glorious* had sailed north for the Norwegian campaign. The Royal Navy wanted four of them back and these were taken away to be used from the aircraft carrier HMS *Eagle*. The logic therefore in using three, with the operational names, *Faith*, *Hope* and *Charity*, was that there would always be one in reserve that could be cannibalised. There was considerable to-ing and fro-ing about the ownership of the aircraft. The Royal Navy wanted to take them back to Egypt but they were used for the first time to intercept ten S79 Italian bombers in an attack at 06.49 on 11 June 1940. Later that day one of the Gladiators would claim the first kill of the campaign.

Photos of the ceremony that took place on 13 September 1942, when Lord Gort presented the George Cross to Sir George Borg, the Chief Justice of Malta. In April 2008 a re-enactment of the handing over of the George Cross took place in Palace Square in Valletta. In the lead-up to the re-enactment the crowd had heard air-raid sirens, the roar of piston-engined aircraft, exploding bombs and BBC reports. The ceremony centred on a dais in the square, draped as it was all those years before with the Union flag. The event in 1942 was bold and brazen, given the circumstances. It took place within days of Operation Pedestal.

On 15 April 1942 King George VI sent a message to Governor Dobbie:

To honour her brave people I award the George Cross to the Island Fortress of Malta, to bear witness to a heroism and a devotion that will be long famous in history.

The award, second only to the Victoria Cross, had normally only ever been awarded to individuals. Accepting the award on behalf of the island, Dobbie replied: 'By God's help Malta will not weaken but will endure until victory is won.'

The George Cross was the highest gallantry award for civilians. In January 1941 the award was created at the insistence of Winston Churchill, who believed that a new medal was needed to recognise the acts of bravery performed by civilians. The Cross can still be seen at Fort St Elmo in Valletta and it still appears on the Maltese flag.

Maltese civilians celebrate the defeat of the Germans and Italians in Tripoli on 23 January 1943. Tripoli was one of the closest Axis-held cities to Malta, lying almost due south from the island. Tripoli had been the port in which Rommel's Afrika Korps had arrived in February 1941 and the base had been used by both the Luftwaffe and the Italian air force to strike at Malta. Tripoli was also a vital supply port for the German and Italian troops, along with Benghazi and Tobruk. The Maltese spontaneously assembled as soon as they heard the BBC announcement: 'It has been officially stated that Tripoli is now in our hands.' There were frantic searches for flags and bunting that had lain hidden away for more than two years. People decorated their balconies, hoisted flags, and bands emerged to entertain the crowds.

Another shot of Maltese civilians and servicemen celebrating the Allies capture of Tripoli in January 1943. On 24 January large groups of people from the outlying villages around Valletta poured into the city. Hundreds attended the early mass at St John's Co-Cathedral, Kingsway, despite the heavy bomb damage, was packed. People moved back and forth, celebrating. Even the servicemen and police were caught up in the celebrations. The two bands in Valletta, for years rivals, combined together and marched up and down the streets.

Some Maltese boys collected as many flags of the different allied nations as they could find, along with Malta's own red-and-white flag. They marched into Palace Square and paraded around the spot where Lord Gort had presented the George Cross to the island. *God Save The King* and the Maltese anthem were played, the flags were dipped and the crowd burst into cheers and applause. Even though the air-raid siren sounded and the anti-aircraft guns opened up, the Maltese crowd did not disperse. In Hamrun an effigy of Mussolini was made and hanged and then burned.

A Maltese boy holding the Union Jack and dressed in a replica RAF uniform surveys the celebrations following the fall of Tripoli in January 1943. With the Germans and Italians being routed in North Africa, and the allies now enjoying air superiority in the Mediterranean, the prospects of a brighter future for Malta were there for all to see. In February 1943 the food ration was increased as more and more merchant ships managed to reach the safety of the Grand Harbour with their precious loads. In the popular poem, *The Tale of the Desert Rats*, the joy of victory was clear:

We fought him where we found him,
And every time got round him;
Which made him lift his sticks and run
For ever to the west.
From Alamein to far Matruh,
Barrani, Derna, Sirte Too;
Till Tripoli came into view
We gave no rest, no rest.
We're chasing, still we're chasing.
We're pounding while he's racing.
We're building up in Tripoli
And looking 'cross the Bay.
While on towards the Mareth Line
The bombers bomb, the star shells shine
They say the weather's clearing fine
On Malta, 'cross the way'.

The Castile guard, now known as the Pjazza Kastilja; also visible is the facade of the Auberge de Castille. It was designed in 1741 by the architect Andrea Belli to enhance a sixteenth-century building that was used by the Knights of St John. It is now the office of the Prime Minister of Malta. During the Second World War the Auberge de Castille was the headquarters of British troops on Malta. During the height of the siege the British devised a flag signal system. Flag stations were established on the governor's palace, which was the government headquarters, and on the Auberge de Castille, the army headquarters. If a red-and-white flag was flown then it meant fighters were heading for the city. A red flag meant bombers. It became custom to wait for a red flag before people fled for the shelters, although many, not being able to see the flags, had to rely on word of mouth. To supplement the signalling system boy scouts were used. They set up miniature signal stations with tiny poles and flags. They watched the main signal stations and hoisted their flags in unison. Many of them put their lives at risk to do so and on no occasion did they signal a false warning. Nearly a thousand of the boy scouts were awarded the Scout's Bronze Cross during the war.

Bibliography

Attard, Joseph. *The Battle of Malta: An Epic True Story of Suffering and Bravery*. Progress Press. 1988.

Austin, Douglas. *Churchill and Malta*. Spellmount. 2006.

Baker, E C R. *The Fighter Aces of the RAF*. Kimber. 1962.

Bradford, Ernle. *Siege: Malta 1940–1943*. Pen & Sword Books. 2003.

Clayton, Tim and Phil Craig. *End of the Beginning: From the Siege of Malta to the Victory at Alamein*. Coronet Books. 2003.

Cull, Brian and Frederick Galea. *Hurricanes Over Malta*. Grub Street. 2002.

Cull, Brian and Frederick Galea. *Spitfires Over Malta*. Grub Street. 2002.

Douglas-Hamilton, James. *The Air Battle for Malta*. Airlife Publishing. 2000.

Forty, George. *The Battle for Malta*. Ian Allan. 2003.

Galea, Frederick R. *Call-Out*. Malta at War Publications. 2002.

Galea, Michael. *Malta: Diary of a War*. Publishers Enterprises Group. 1992.

McAulay, Lex. *Against All Odds*. Hutchinson. 1989.

McCaffery, Dan. *Hell Island*. James Lorimer. 1998.

Ministry of Information. *The Air Battle of Malta*. HMSO. 1944.

Hogan, George. *Malta: The Triumphant Years 1940–1943*. Progress Press. Malta. 1988.

Holland, James. *Fortress Malta*. Orion. 2003.

Leighton, Frank. *Frayed Lifelines: A Siege Survivor's Story*. Trafford. 2003.

Lucas, Laddie. *Malta: The Thorn in Rommel's Side*. Stanley Paul. 1992.

Roger, Anthony. *Battle Over Malta*. Sutton Publishing. 2000.

Roger, Anthony. *185: The Malta Squadron*. The History Press. 2005.

Sutherland, Jon and Diane Canwell. *Air War Malta*. Pen & Sword Aviation. 2008.

Williamson, David G. *Malta Besieged 1940–1942*. Pen & Sword Military. 2007.

Wragg, David. *Malta: The Last Great Siege*. Leo Cooper. 2003.